Lighthearted Life

Simple strategies
to live a joy-filled life
even in the stormiest times

By Dianne Callahan

Published by Lighthearted Life

LightheartedLife.org

ISBN:
9781728919645

Table of Contents

Coloring Pages

I love coloring! For me, coloring is like meditation, helping me feel calm and relaxed. It allows me to do something a little bit creative without a lot of artistic talent. It's also a great way to reflect on something you have read while you create something beautiful.

I hope you enjoy the coloring pages and inspirational quotes we included in this book!

Sometimes the greatest storms
bring out the greatest beauty...
Life can be a storm, but your
hope is a rainbow and your
friends and family are the gold.

Steve Maraboli

Dedication

This little book is dedicated to all of the delicious, funny, insightful, courageous, encouraging, and amazing friends God has blessed me with, especially...

Jean Moody, BFF and life soulmate

And my Sophias:

Jill Wagner
spiritual teacher and sister of my heart

Joan Sieczkowski
our voice of wisdom and humor

Cindy Sabato
our sweet seeker and supporter

and our beloved Carolyn Taylor
who taught us all how to love fiercely and live for today

Because true friends
encourage you, inspire you
and believe in your dreams
even when you are afraid
to believe in them yourself.

Foreword

As an oncologist specializing in the treatment of blood cancers, every day I have to tell people the scariest three words in the English language - "you have cancer." And every day I put patients through intense therapies including risky bone marrow and stem cell transplants to try to save their lives.

Over the past 20 years, I have seen first-hand the impact a patient's outlook has on his or her recovery and long-term survival. I firmly believe that hope and laughter can be as important to a positive medical outcome as the chemotherapy and other treatments I prescribe.

Few of my patients have brought as much hope and laughter to their treatment as Dianne Callahan has. I've known Dianne now for more than 11 years. I met her at what was likely one of the lowest points in her life. She had just turned 43 and I had to tell her she had Stage IV Diffuse Large B-cell Lymphoma. What I didn't tell her that day in the hospital is that she was literally at death's door and I was not confident at all that we could save her life.

Since that day, Dianne has been through three fights with her cancer and has undergone two stem cell transplants, most recently with an unrelated donor's cells. She's had a number of life-altering complications from her transplants, but she is determined to remain upbeat and hopeful even when she physically feels the worst.

I have watched as Dianne has turned her illness into a mission to help other people not only survive cancer, but thrive. She raises money for cancer research. She volunteers to help other patients prepare for their transplants. She travels the country speaking to groups to encourage people to choose hope and joy in the midst of their own challenges.

Mostly, Dianne makes people smile and gives them a positive moment in their day. We love when Dianne comes in for her follow-up appointments. She fills the office with sunshine and makes all of us – patients and the medical team – feel good. She has figured out the prescription for finding joy even in the darkest times.

Dr. Leonardo Farol
Hematologist Oncologist

Dianne and Dr. Len Farol celebrating five years of survival post stem cell transplant at the annual City of Hope Bone Marrow Transplant Reunion, May, 2018.

Section One: Happiness Fitness

When it comes to our physical health, based on our DNA each of us falls somewhere on the fitness continuum, between sweatsuits on one end and red bikinis on the other. While we can thank our genes for our baseline, decades-old science has shown us that there are many things we can do to move closer to the healthier, red bikini, side of life. Things like eating a balanced diet, exercising regularly, getting enough sleep, and drinking lots of water.

Did you know that our DNA also places us on a continuum of emotional health somewhere between a stormy outlook and a sunshiny worldview? You can thank great Uncle Harold for your tendency to jump to the worst case scenario. But the GREAT news is that in the past 15-20 years, scientific research has uncovered concrete things we can do daily to move closer to the sunnier side of life as we strengthen our happiness fitness.

Happiness Fitness

WHAT IS HAPPINESS ANYWAY?

We all have deeply personal, and often quite different, definitions of what happiness is, but scientists define happiness as a combination of how satisfied you are with your life plus how good you feel on a day-to-day basis.

So, what's your happiness score right now? Give yourself a rating between 0 (totally disagree) and 5 (totally agree) as you read the following statements:

1. In general, I consider myself a happy person   ____
2. I am more happy than most people I know   ____
3. In tough times I can usually see a bright spot   ____
4. I can be happy even when things don't go my way   ____

Average your answers to get your Happiness Score   [   ]

Are you good with your score? Would you like it to be higher?

Happiness Fitness

SCIENTIFICALLY PROVEN BENEFITS TO BECOMING HAPPIER

According to researchers, happy people enjoy myriad physical health benefits including:

- lower rates of cardiovascular disease
- enhanced immunity
- better ability to maintain a healthy diet
- healing faster after injuries
- longer life!

 # Happiness Fitness

YOUR HAPPINESS ISN'T JUST ABOUT YOU

It is easy to think of the pursuit of a happier life as a purely selfish effort. But the truth is, happy people make a huge positive imprint on others. (Except those people - you know the ones - who get irritated by happy folks, but that's a whole other book!)

Here are some of the ways happy people make the world better:

- they are more productive at work
- they are more creative problem solvers
- they typically have deep, committed relationships
- they are more likely to help others
- they often volunteer in their community
- they are more likely to donate to charitable causes

Happiness Fitness

WHAT HAPPINESS ISN'T

There is no secret science of "happiology." Difficult times come into all of our lives and simply enjoining others to "turn that frown upside down" can sometimes do more harm than good.

Happiness is NOT:

* pretending that everything is AWESOME all of the time
* feeling like bursting into song every minute of the day
* refusing to acknowledge the negative things in the world
* having all the _____ you could want (money, time, Instagram followers, etc.)
* the reward of a final destination (when I retire, I will finally be happy)

Happiness Fitness

HOW MUCH CAN YOU REALLY CHANGE?

Remember the physical and emotional continuums we talked about at the beginning of this section?

Researchers determined that where your genetic make-up places you on the emotional continuum is responsible for approximately 50% of your ability to be happier. I know that seems to mean a lot is out of your control, but stick with me.

Another 10% is determined by your daily circumstances. Contrary to what advertisers tell us, that fancy new car makes us happy, yes, but only for a short amount of time. Soon enough it becomes the same old car and we are off looking for a new shiny object to pin our happiness on.

Happiness Fitness

SO WHAT ABOUT THE OTHER 40%?

This is where it gets amazing! Forty percent of our happiness is controlled by our thoughts, words, actions and behaviors!

Think about your favorite pie. What's yours? Mine is classic pumpkin (usually cold and for breakfast). Imagine instead of a skinny little piece, you get a slice that is 40% of the whole pie! That's a lot of pie goodness!

40% gives you a lot to work with when it comes to making a difference in your level of happiness. Happiness is a skill that can be built with consistent practice. Each of us has the ability to increase our happiness fitness and take control of how fulfilling our life is.

"A flower blossoms
for its own joy."

Oscar Wilde

Happiness Fitness

HAPPINESS WORKOUT: TAKE CARE OF YOURSELF

If you're looking for a quick happiness fix you may not want to hear this, but the first step in upping your happiness game is self care. When we do the things we know we should for our overall health, we increase our happiness, too. Some of it has to do with those endorphins that get released when we take a walk, and some of it is due to the general goodness we feel when we deem ourselves important enough to take care of.

So be sure to tackle the basics:

- feed your body good, nutritious food most of the time
- get some movement into each day
- don't be so quick to give up the sleep you need
- drink the water your body and brain crave to function well
- schedule time for relaxation (a massage, reading, meditation, whatever works for you)

Happiness Fitness

HAPPINESS WORKOUT: INVEST IN RELATIONSHIPS

Few factors have as much impact on our lives as our sense of connection to other people. Did you know that feelings of loneliness and isolation are more detrimental to your health and longevity than smoking 15 cigarettes a day? That's almost a PACK A DAY.

Additionally, people who feel disconnected are 3-5 times more likely to experience stroke, cancer, heart attack and suicide.

Taking time - no, let's say it right - MAKING time to spend with our friends, family, neighbors and co-workers is vital not only to our health but also to our happiness. Getting to really know others and letting them really know you (warts and all) is an investment that will pay dividends today when times are good, and someday in the future when you truly need the love and support of your closest allies.

Happiness Fitness

HAPPINESS WORKOUT: SAVOR THE GOOD STUFF

You get more happiness out of good things when you become an expert at really savoring them. Savoring is a way to imprint that experience on your heart and mind so that you can recollect it and re-experience all the great feelings again and again. It's more than memories - it's a sensory experience. Savoring experiences can make us more hopeful and more grateful and reduces stress and depression.

Here are some ways to savor the good stuff:

+ focus all of your senses on the moment - what do you see, touch, smell, taste, hear?
+ linger - don't be so quick to move on to the next thing
+ say a prayer of gratitude for the experience
+ share the experience with others (this is one of the best ways to engage with social media, in my opinion)

Happiness Fitness

HAPPINESS WORKOUT: STOP DOING THIS STUFF

There are some things we do that are genuine, bona-fide happiness killers. Sometimes we don't even realize we're doing them. If we truly want to increase our happiness fitness we have to get extremely good at identifying our own happiness killers and stopping them in their tracks. Here are some killers:

- comparing ourselves to others (Facebook, I'm looking at you)
- ruminating on things that we don't like / didn't go our way
- holding on to resentment and/or withholding forgiveness
- assuming that things others do are on purpose to hurt us
- ...anything you need to add?

I literally say "NO" out loud when I catch myself falling into my own happiness-killing thoughts and behaviors. Let's practice that strategy right now. Just say no to your happiness killers! Catching ourselves when we fall into those old patterns is the first step in establishing behaviors that better serve us.

18

Happiness Fitness

HAPPINESS WORKOUT: MAKE TIME FOR YOUR JOY

Only you know what really makes you happy. What are the activities that give you a perma-smile? The ones where you completely lose track of time? Those things that get your heart racing and shake away the worries of the day? DO THEM!

Oh, yeah, you don't have time for that stuff, right? Here are a few strategies for fitting joy into your life - no matter how busy you are:

- schedule time for joy right on your calendar just like any other important appointment
- set your alarm 30 or 60 minutes earlier to practice joy
- look for tasks you can delegate to others
- ask a trusted friend to be your joy accountability partner
- look for potential time-wasters (like watching mindless TV or surfing the Web) that you can cut down to free up time to do what really makes you happy

Making time for joy in your life is so worth it. And it doesn't have to be a two-week trip to Bali - you can get a happiness boost from joyful activities big and small.

On the grid below, chart some of the activities that bring you joy based on the time and effort it takes to do them and the happiness boost you get from them. Look - I got you started!

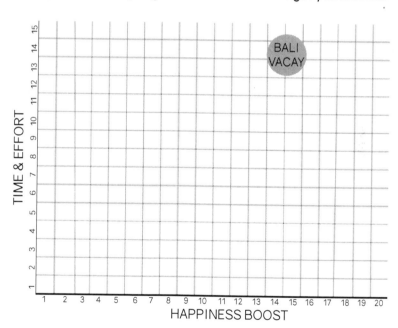

Happiness Fitness

HAPPINESS WORKOUT: MANAGE A BAD DAY / BAD MOOD

Even the happiest people get hit with a bad day on occasion.
All kinds of things can happen that make a day truly suck.
Remember that bad days or bad moods don't have to control
you. I know it is much easier said than done, but there are proven
tactics for managing the inevitable bad mood. The first is to put
strategies in place so you can call on them to help keep a day or
mood from spiraling out of control.

Here are a few ideas:

- When you are really in a funk, set a timer and let yourself
  wallow in that bad mood. 10 minutes, 30 minutes ... the
  important thing is to shake it off and do something else
  when the timer goes off
- Make a list of joy activities that will help you shake off a bad
  mood - for example, I can never stay upset when I'm playing
  with my sweet dog Dagny!

Happiness Fitness

HAPPINESS WORKOUT: SAY "YES" ... AND SOMETIMES "NO"

It can be hard to say "no" to others' requests for our time and energy. Everyone is invested in us living up to expectations - especially ourselves! I'm not suggesting that you say "no" to everyone and everything. But, before you say "yes" to a request (that may sound suspiciously like a demand) think about what you're saying "no" to for yourself or your family.

We have only so much time and, most importantly, mental and physical energy. When you say "yes" to an event or task, are you saying "no" to your wish to spend more time with your kids or grandkids? Are you saying "no" to doing something else that you know will really bring you joy / peace / meaning / happiness?

Rarely will someone jump in and say "no" for you. That's your call. If it's not a resounding enthusiastic "yes!" for you, then it just might be an equally resounding (and guilt-free) "no."

Happiness Fitness

HAPPINESS WORKOUT: SMILE

Smiling is powerful!

As smart as your miraculous brain is, it can be fooled by a few things. And one of those things is your smile. When you paste a smile on your face, even when you don't feel like smiling, your brain "reads" the placement of your facial muscles and uses them to infer how you feel. A smile, the brain knows, means you are happy. So it starts a little feel-good party by releasing happiness "cocktails" into your system like dopamine, endorphins and serotonin. And those little suckers are famous for reducing stress, bringing down your heart rate, and lifting up your mood, which actually makes you *feel* better.

Are you smiling now?

Happiness Fitness

MAKING IT STICK - JOURNALING

What stood out for you in this chapter? What things do you plan
to try or to do differently to increase your happiness fitness?

_____

_____

_____

_____

_____

_____

_____

_____

_____

_____

_____

Section Two: The Art & Science of Gratitude

If I told you there was something you could do that would provide physical, psychological AND social benefits in your day-to-day life, would you do it? Research studies have shown that establishing a consistent gratitude practice is the key to reaping all of those great benefits - today and into the future.

Today, scientists are exploring the concepts of psychological well-being and emotional prosperity. (Isn't **that** a wonderful term?) And what they're finding is that our feelings of joy and satisfaction with life can be directly linked to our level of gratitude.

Some lucky people are just naturally grateful. They are truly thankful for their blessings and are able to see the silver lining in almost any situation. Some of us, however, need to commit to a regular practice to help us live in that attitude of gratitude. Read on for ways to establish - or uplevel - your own gratitude activities.

The Art & Science of Gratitude

BIOLOGY AND PSYCHOLOGY - HOW YOUR BRAIN WORKS

Many decades ago, Dr. Brian Hebb, a pioneer in neuro-psychology, studied the brain looking for biological explanations for numerous psychological phenomena.

He determined that whenever we think a thought or have a feeling or physical sensation, thousands of neurons "light up" in our brain and form an internal neural network. And our brain learns to trigger those neural networks with repetitive thinking. These thought patterns wire our brains to react positively or negatively to the situations we are presented.

It's a lot like pop-up ads on your computer. After you have been "thinking" about or searching for something online, those items seem to keep popping up in your sidebars and social media. Your brain does that, too.

 # The Art & Science of Gratitude

INTENSELY, REPEATEDLY AND REWARDINGLY

Current knowledge of the brain holds that we are constantly in a state of neurogenesis - the process of cellular renewal that keeps our brains developing new neurons and connections until we die.

Those connections are strengthened by everything we do intensely, repeatedly and rewardingly.

* Intensely (with rapt attention)
* Repeatedly (with focused repetition)
* Rewardingly (with some kind of positive effect)

Several studies have shown physical changes in the brain after just a few weeks of intense, repeated and rewarding practice.

The Art & Science of Gratitude

SO WHAT ARE YOU FOCUSING ON?

If we spend our time and energy worrying, ruminating and venting about the things that might not go our way, we are actively creating negative "pop-up ads" in our brains. And each time something not-so-good happens, those thoughts pop up right away and make us feel even more victimized. But the flip side is also true. If we regularly focus our thoughts on what is going well in our lives - what we are thankful for - our brains learn to easily bring positive expectations to the surface and to more deeply appreciate positive experiences.

I think that talking about our problems is our greatest addiction. But we **can** break this habit and learn to talk about our joys. When we change our perspective, we are in effect rewriting our brain chemistry.

The Art & Science of Gratitude

PROCESSING LIFE THROUGH A LENS OF THANKFULNESS

No amount of positive thinking can change the truth that life includes ups and downs and some real gut-wrenching suffering.

Processing a difficult life experience through a grateful lens does not mean denying pain, fear, stress, and sadness. Those are all righteous feelings and should not be ignored or "happied" over.

But, you **can** choose the option of seeing whatever good there is in the situation. Look for possible positive outcomes. Remind yourself that somewhere, someone has it even worse than you do. Find ways to transform an obstacle into a potential gain.

This is a tactic called reframing. Wisdom? Strength? A new path more right for you? A way to help someone else going through what you went through? These are all possible positive outcomes that can bring meaning (and, yes, gratitude) to our challenges.

The heart of man
is very much like the sea,
it has its storms,
it has its tides,
and in its depths
it has its pearls too.

Vincent Van Gogh

The Art & Science of Gratitude

DEVELOPING YOUR GRATITUDE MUSCLE

There are many ways to create a gratitude practice to help you make thankfulness a habit. One of the most studied practices is keeping a gratitude journal.

Some people jot down three things they are grateful for each day. Some write a weekly review of all the things they have to be thankful for. Some use an app on their phone to type in their thoughts. Some use the tried-and-true pen and paper method. Some start their day with their gratitude reflection and some focus on their blessings just before bed.

It doesn't matter how you do it - the important thing is to create a practice that feels right for you and becomes a good, happy habit. And if journaling isn't your thing, check out the following ways to practice gratitude.

The Art & Science of Gratitude

GRATITUDE PRACTICE: GRATITUDE JAR

An easy way to recognize the things you are grateful for is with a gratitude jar. The idea is to write on a slip of paper something you are grateful for that day and place it in your gratitude jar or box (any container will do). You can do this alone or your whole family can get involved. You can get super creative decorating your container.

Then decide how often you will look through the jar to be reminded of the good things that happen every day. You can do this weekly, monthly, quarterly or annually.

I like to date my slips of paper. One really fun way to do this is to use one of those page-a-day desk calendars. At the end of each day you can just tear off the sheet and write the things you are grateful for on the back!

# The Art & Science of Gratitude

GRATITUDE PRACTICE: CAPTURING GRATITUDE

When was the last time you didn't have your phone with you?
I can't even remember! Our phones go with us everywhere.

Use the camera in your phone to capture gratitude. Take a
photo each day of something that delights you - something
that makes you happy to be alive.

You can store the photos on your phone, download them to
a gratitude file on your computer, or upload them to your
favorite social media platforms. You can even make a book at
the end of the year to celebrate your favorite moments.

This practice helps us to look for and see the good things in
our life every day!

The Art & Science of Gratitude

GRATITUDE PRACTICE: GRATITUDE WALK

Did you know that when we take a walk the positive impact can be seen on a brain scan? The endorphins released after a 20-minute walk cause parts of our brains to literally light up.

Now imagine if the purpose of our walk was to meditate on all of the things we have to be thankful for and to notice the beauty all around us. Talk about rewriting our brain chemistry!

 # The Art & Science of Gratitude

GRATITUDE PRACTICE: GRATITUDE COLLAGE

Have you read about vision boards or created one yourself? Vision boards are a great way to keep your dreams and intentions right in front of you every day.

This practice works in the same way. You simply create a collage of the things you are deeply grateful for. You can use personal pictures or you can cut images out of magazines. You can use words and phrases, scripture, or cards you've received - really the possibilities are endless! Your collage can be created online and printed out or you can attach your images to a foam board or a bulletin board.

The important thing is to keep your collage where you can see it every day, so even on the most challenging days you are reminded of the many things you have to be truly thankful for.

 # The Art & Science of Gratitude

GRATITUDE PRACTICE: A-Z LIST

Do you ever have trouble sleeping? Nights where the hamsters in your head just won't stop running on that dang wheel? I know I do.

When I can't sleep I challenge myself to alphabetize things. It can be types of flowers, cars, movies or even countries. (Thank goodness for Qatar!) The idea is to get your brain focused on something other than those hamsters but not something too engrossing that will keep you from drifting off to sleep.

That's what gave me the idea for this gratitude practice. Try listing something you are thankful for to go with each letter of the alphabet. You can do this in writing or try it next time you can't get to sleep - I guarantee you will have sweet dreams!

 # The Art & Science of Gratitude

GRATITUDE PRACTICE: REVERSE BUCKET LIST

Many people have a bucket list in their heads or in writing of all the things they want to do, see and accomplish before they kick the proverbial bucket. These lists are great motivators but they can sometimes have the opposite effect, leaving us feeling stressed out or thinking we are falling behind.

The concept of the reverse bucket list is to take some time and reflect on all of the great things you have *already* seen, done and accomplished. When you gather all of these outstanding life experiences into one amazing list, you can experience a deep feeling of gratitude for the many ways life has already blessed you. And you just might see that no matter how many more things you have to check off on your bucket list, you are in the middle of a pretty wonderful life!

# The Art & Science of Gratitude

GRATITUDE PRACTICE: JUST SAY THANK YOU

I have heard it said that gratitude begins in our hearts and seeks expression in acts of kindness. When someone does an act of kindness for you, don't forget to say thank you. And the more specific you are about the act itself, the giver's good intentions, and the impact it had on you the better.

Gratitude thrives on specificity. When you take the time to specifically thank someone, you are not only making their day, you are confirming in your own spirit that the world contains good people who are kind and giving. You are affirming that good things happen to you. You get as much, if not more, from the act of expressing your thanks.

So, jot down a note and drop it in the mail. Pick up the phone and make that call. Post a photo on social media and tag the person you are thanking. Send that text. Just get thanking!

The Art & Science of Gratitude

GRATITUDE PRACTICE: HAVE TO / GET TO

"The things you take for granted, someone else is praying for."
This stopped me in my tracks the first time I read it.

How many times have I complained about having to vacuum
and dust, do laundry or get the dinner dishes done? How many
people would give almost anything to have a roof over their
head, clothes to wear and healthy food to feed their kids?

We can all benefit by learning to replace every "have to" we
say with "get to" - this one small switch can change our entire
perspective on the privilege we have of living.

Consider: I get to go to work. I get to go shopping. I get to go
to my child's open house. Getting to is pretty great!

The Art & Science of Gratitude

THANKING OUTSIDE THE BOX

You know that Garth Brooks song "Unanswered Prayers"?
It's about the blessing of not getting what you thought you
really wanted. It could be the theme song for the concept of
thanking outside the box, because sometimes there's a much
greater plan in the works than the one we cling so tightly to.

My husband, Chuck, was laid off from a job that he loved that
had great stability and benefits. It was a huge hit to the gut
and shook us to the core financially. But now, two years later,
we know that losing that job actually saved his life.

That loss led to a new job with a different health plan, which
led to a colonoscopy that had never been done when Chuck
entered his 50s, which led to more tests and the final diagno-
sis that he had **both** colon cancer and kidney cancer.

The Art & Science of Gratitude

Chuck successfully underwent surgery to remove all of the cancer from his colon and his entire right kidney. Blessedly, he is cancer-free today. Each of these cancers could have gone undetected for a long time and ultimately been fatal if he hadn't gotten a new doctor because of having to get a new job.

Did we jump for joy the day he was laid off? Could/would you? Of course not. But these kinds of stories remind us that if we are willing to look, we can find a reason to be thankful even in the worst situations.

I once saw a sign that read "When things go wrong, take a moment to be thankful for the many things that are still going right." Patience, faith, hope ... it might take all of these, but if we can find a way to remain thankful in the darkest times, we will eventually see the greater plan play out.

# The Art & Science of Gratitude

MAKING IT STICK - JOURNALING

What stood out for you in this chapter? What things do you plan
to try or to do to grow your gratitude practice?

Section Three: Get More FUN in Your Life

When we were kids we played and explored and laughed every day. Pretty much everything we did was fun (except, perhaps, for eating peas and going to the dentist). So what happened?

Society and rules and fear of looking stupid happened. Bills and babies and bosses with sticks up their butts happened. We are taught that life is too serious to waste time having fun. But I would say that because life is serious we MUST seek out fun and laughter. Science agrees.

The benefits associated with good old-fashioned fun are plentiful: stress reduction; more refreshing sleep which ups your energy level; improved coping ability; better memory and concentration; increased creativity and productivity.

With all of these proven benefits, it would be downright irresponsible NOT to try to get more fun in your life!

 # Get More Fun In Your Life

HAVING MORE FUN STARTS IN YOUR HEAD

The Oxford English Dictionary defines fun as "amusement, especially lively or playful." The concepts of fun and play are often used interchangeably.

An essential way to get more fun in your life is to cultivate a playful outlook or mindset. That starts with actively eschewing the societal thinking that playfulness is childish. Practice not taking yourself too seriously. Seek to infuse spontaneity and curiosity into your days. Question authority. Get into some mischief and do things you're not "supposed" to do. Look up and around more. Laugh at yourself. Sing. Dance. Stop worrying about what others may think. (Pro tip: they're probably wishing they were having as much fun as you!)

Playfulness is a mindset AND a skill which means it can be developed with intentional practice.

Get More Fun In Your Life

AWAKENING YOUR PLAYFUL SPIRIT

We are taught to take life seriously, to seek success and pres-
tige. This will make people like and respect you, we are told.
But did you know that people who have a spirit of playfulness
have a magnetic quality that people seek to be around?

One of the best ways to awaken your own playful spirit is
simply to engage in a lighthearted way with other people.
Notice all the cat pictures at the receptionist's desk and ask if
she got the crazy cat lady starter kit. Banter a bit with the guy
in the Green Bay Packers shirt (extra points if you are wearing
another team's shirt). Look for ways to interact; to connect; to
share a smile or a laugh.

Sometimes your efforts will land on deaf ears. The other
person might not be having the best day and might not be in
the mood to smile. That's okay. Keep smiling.

"Laughter is
a sunbeam
of the soul."

Thomas Mann

# Get More Fun In Your Life

WHAT IS YOUR KIND OF FUN?

The beloved writer C.S. Lewis once said, "Have fun, even if it's not the same kind of fun everyone else is having."

So what's your kind of fun? Most adults can't even remember what they used to like to do. Or they've outgrown things that were fun in the past but haven't gotten around to looking for new things to enjoy. Sound like you? Try these easy steps for figuring out your kind of fun.

Step one: Make a list of things that were fun when you were a kid. Next, go over your list and highlight anything that still sounds appealing (or, let's face it, physically doable).

Step two: Do a Google search for "fun ideas for adults" - you're looking for fun things you may want to try (like salsa dancing, or salsa making). Once you have some ideas, high-light the activities that sound the most interesting.

50

Get More Fun In Your Life

NEXT, GO HAVE FUN!

"But I'm so busy," you say, "I have all these chores and work and deadlines and responsibilities, you see." Me too.

Here's where our work strategies can be used to help us get more fun in our lives as well as be successful in our careers:

1. Set a goal to play more. Is your goal two hours a week of fun activities? Two hours a day? A month? Whatever it is, set a goal and measure your progress. Rewards don't hurt either.

2. Schedule fun. Just like meetings or mammograms, put your fun activities right on your calendar. Fun times matter that much to your health, and success and well-being.

3. Go for the combo. Add fun to activities you already do. Skip the gym and take a walk with a friend. Put on disco music and shake your groove thing while you do the dishes. Get creative!

Get More Fun In Your Life

PLANNING FOR SPONTANEITY IS NOT AN OXYMORON

Although play often happens spontaneously, planning time for play ensures that it **can** happen.

My dad was a great one for spontaneous fun. Every once in a while, he'd tell us kids to "come along for the ride." No matter how much we'd ask, he wouldn't tell us where we were headed until we got there or figured it out ourselves. Sometimes it was a ride up in the mountains behind our house. Often it was a quick trip to Baskin Robbins for ice cream cones. One unforgettable time it was a day at Disneyland for my sister and me!

Schedule a day of spontaneous fun with your romantic partner, kids, grandkids, or friends with no planned activities, no goals or intended outcomes other than having fun. Set a starting point and then toss a coin to decide where to head next. Follow the curve of the road and see what there is to see. Make memories. Go along for the ride.

Get More Fun In Your Life

SPEND TIME WITH PEOPLE WHO ARE BETTER AT FUN

Athletes know that the way to get better at playing a sport is to play against people who are better than you. This is doubly true when the sport in question is having fun. So, get out there and apprentice yourself to an expert.

Who's your most playful friend or family member? Schedule some time to hang out with them and let them be a role model.

Spend time with a kid in your life. Talk about learning from a pro how to have fun! Even an empty box is fun to a kid - it's a car...it's a pirate ship! Soak in their imaginative ways to play.

Play with you dog or cat (or borrow one for the afternoon). Have you ever seen a dog in a bad mood? Dogs are always ready to romp and play. And even the most aloof "catitudinal" feline will leap around when a piece of string is dangled.

Get More Fun In Your Life

SOME FUN IDEAS TO GET YOU STARTED

- Do something physically challenging
- Take a class in something you've always wanted to try
- Next time it rains, grab your boots and take a walk
- Create a playlist of songs that make you want to dance
- Take a weekend road trip
- Try ziplining or parasailing - both are safe but exhilarating!
- Go to the drive-in movies in your PJs
- Schedule a game night with friends
- Recreate a scene from your favorite movie
- Get your friends to hit a country western bar and take a line dancing lesson
- Go horseback riding
- Have a slumber party
- Explore your inner artist at a "sip and paint" party
- Learn to expertly deliver three great jokes
- Set a timer for 25 minutes to do something fun with no distractions

Get More FUN In Your Life

MAKING IT STICK - JOURNALING

What stood out for you in this chapter? What things do you plan
to try or to do to get more fun in your life?

Section Four: Up Your Love Game

When we hear the word "love" our minds seem to instantly think of the romantic type of love - your basic Hallmark Channel fare. But there are so many other types of love! There's love of oneself, brotherly love or friendship, family love as in parents for their children, and agape love - the universal, altruistic love for strangers, community and nature.

I was once in a stem cell transplant survivor group where we were asked how we planned to leave our legacy. Some people spoke of trusts and wills, some talked of writing letters to their kids before they underwent the transplant process. When it was my turn, I blurted out "I guess I've just concentrated on upping my love game" which generated lots of questions. What I meant, I explained, is that I want to make sure that everyone I love knows it - and they know the impact they've made on my life. And I want to do a better job of spreading love and kindness in the world while I am here.

Is it time for you to up your own love game?

Up Your Love Game

DON'T ASSUME THEY KNOW HOW YOU FEEL

I think one of the biggest mistakes we make (and potentially our biggest regret) is assuming that the people we love KNOW it. We tell ourselves "of course he knows I love him - I'm his mother." Or "she must know how proud I am." Or "I'm sure they know how much I appreciate them."

But HOW do they know these things? Osmosis? ESP? When we care about someone, it is our responsibility to be sure they know it.

I don't think anyone ever really suffered under the burden of being told too often that they were loved. But I am certain that many, many people suffer in sad and painful silence wondering what they really mean to the people in their lives. So tell them. Show them. Be specific. It will bring joy to them and to you.

Up Your Love Game

SPEAKING THE RIGHT LANGUAGE

Dr. Gary Chapman is a pastor, author, speaker, and radio host. He regularly discusses the concepts he wrote about in his book "The Five Love Languages" and they have had a huge impact on my own and thousands of people's relationships with spouses, family members, colleagues and friends. Have you read it? No? Go order it on Amazon - I'll wait!

Dr. Chapman teaches that there are five distinct love languages: words of affirmation, acts of service, quality time, giving and receiving gifts, and physical touch.

His teaching opened my eyes to the fact that when it comes to expressing love and receiving expressions of love, there is a possibility that you and your loved one, friend, family member or colleague might be speaking totally different languages.

Up Your Love Game

GETTING THE TRANSLATION RIGHT

If you really want to connect with someone in your life, you need to know how to speak in their language. But how can you tell which love language someone speaks? Dr. Chapman has a simple assessment tool on his website that is easy to complete.

Or you might use the strategies below to determine which language(s) are spoken by your family members, friends and colleagues:

- Ask them
- Observe how they interact with others
- Take note of how they express appreciation to you - we tend to "speak" in the language we are most comfortable with

Up Your Love Game

USE YOUR WORDS

Below are some examples of ways to use words to show your love and appreciation for others:

- Tell your nearest and dearest what you most appreciate about them and the impact they've made in your life
- Send a heartfelt note, text, voicemail or email
- Give kudos about them to others
- Introduce people like my friend DeAnna does by sharing one of their best traits that you admire in them
- Put sticky notes with what you love about them where they will find them
- Use milestones - "We've been colleagues for 12 years and here are a dozen things I appreciate about you"
- Practice saying those three little words. It might make you uncomfortable at first, but think of how sad you would both be if you didn't make sure they knew how you felt about them.

"There are souls
in this world who have the
gift of finding joy everywhere,
and leaving it behind them
when they go."

Frederick William Faber

Up Your Love Game

GIFTS FROM THE HEART

Gifts are mementos that we keep to remember the kindness of the giver. Gifts don't have to be lavish or expensive to be meaningful (the best, most loving and thoughtful gift I ever received was a GPS). Here are a few ideas for heartfelt gift giving:

- ◆ Give them unexpected gifts when it's not a holiday or their birthday - "I saw this and thought of you."
- ◆ Support causes they care deeply about
- ◆ Give something they've admired from your own collection
- ◆ Give them a chance to do something they've always wanted to try (painting, parasailing, cooking)
- ◆ Give them a copy of the book you are reading so you can discuss it together
- ◆ Bring them flowers or send flowers to someone they love
- ◆ Make something for them

Up Your Love Game

TIME IN A BOTTLE

Time is truly our greatest commodity. It's something we never think we have enough of. And there will come a day when it will run out for each of us. So make time to spend with the people who are most important to you - get it on the calendar and don't miss out! Here are some ideas:

- Show up for them - don't miss the occasion, birthday, etc.
- Do something they like to do even if it's not your cup of tea
- Travel together
- Go for a walk together or to the gym or to the grocery store
- Meet for a picnic lunch
- Take a class or a workshop together
- Ask them about their childhood, favorite memories, best gift they ever received, something they are most proud of, what they wanted to be when they grew up, the craziest thing they ever did - ask them and then really listen

Up Your Love Game

SERVING OTHERS

Helping and serving our loved ones is a wonderful way to show we care. Some people aren't as comfortable with saying "I love you" but they are ready to help! They fix the dryer or dinner or a flat tire, and the underlying message is they care.

- Don't just offer to help - jump in and do it
- Be reliable - let them know they can count on you
- Be good to the people who are important to them
- Help them do something they are dreading
- Use your best skills for them (event planning, organizing, closet cleaning, computer upgrades, you name it!)
- Help them make their deepest dreams happen
- Be an accountability partner
- Watch their kids or pets - whatever gives them time

Up Your Love Game

PHYSICAL TOUCH

We've all read the reports about how babies who aren't held and touched often fail to thrive. Did you know that adults need physical touch as much as those babies? We humans are made for touching. In fact, hugs are scientifically proven to boost the immune system, lower blood pressure and decrease stress.

Unfortunately, many of us are suffering from a real deficit in getting the touch we need to be our healthiest and happiest. Here are some ideas to help:

◆ Hug it out!
◆ Hold their hand or pat their back
◆ Give them the gift of a spa treatment - a massage or facial, a mani/pedi - these are all relaxing ways for people to experience touch

Up Your Love Game

"LISTEN" IN THEIR LANGUAGE

Communication is a two-way street. One person sends the message and the other receives it. What happens when someone is trying to send a message of love in the only language they know? If you speak another language, you may miss their message and you could hurt the person who is doing something *they* think is the ultimate way to show they care.

But what if you were able to become multilingual in the love languages? What if you could learn to "listen" as well as speak in their language?

Your husband putting gas in your car? Love. An unexpected gift in the mail from a friend? Love. Your brother driving you to doctor's appointments? Love. They may not be speaking your language but they are definitely communicating love.

Up Your Love Game

LOVING YOURSELF

The one person we will spend our entire life with is ourself. Life can be very painful if you don't love (or even like) that person. Many of us carry around an invisible burden - it's like an extremely heavy backpack filled with things like fear, shame, regret, pain, loss, and anger. Sound familiar?

While your backpack might be invisible to others, it sure is easy to see the impact it has in your life and your happiness. When you hold that backpack so close, it makes an excellent barrier between yourself and other people. It blocks love: love for yourself; love for others; love **from** others.

It's also exhausting to carry that heavy backpack everywhere you go. It leaves you too worn out to have fun, to reach out to others, to take good care of yourself. Its weight wears away joy. And hope. And peace.

Up Your Love Game

FORGIVING YOURSELF

Each of us has been created for good things (great things even) by a creator (God, the universe, or whatever reference you prefer) whose sole business is love. We can choose to accept that infinite love and live into it by treating ourselves with love. And kindness. And, yes, forgiveness.

But, how? Well, it usually isn't something that happens overnight. It happens day-by-day as we treat ourselves better - like the way we would treat our best friend, or the best friend we wish we had - by being gentle and kind and loving with our thoughts and words about ourselves.

Rewrite your story and give it the hero's ending. "Yes, she made a mess of things, but she persevered and in the end she saved the world!" Or even better, she saved herself and was a better friend, partner, and parent, choosing to live with joy and love.

Up Your Love Game

CAN YOU SET DOWN THAT HEAVY BACKPACK?

Only you can let that backpack go. Sometimes we don't want to because it might leave us vulnerable. We might worry that there's nothing better out there for us. Setting aside the back-pack isn't about other people at all - it's about choosing to love yourself with all your flaws, mistakes and regrets.

And the very first step is to forgive yourself. Most of us are just little baby bunnies trying to get through life. We make the best decisions we can with what we know in that moment. Looking back, do we wish we had done some things differ-ently? Would we go back and change some things? I can only speak for myself, and the answer is YES! But just because we wish our past was different, are we unforgivable, doomed to pay for our mistakes every day in the loss of love and kindness to ourselves? The answer is a vehement NO!

Up Your Love Game

WHEN WE KNOW BETTER WE DO BETTER

One day, that backpack will feel so heavy, so burdensome, and so very unnecessary. You will want nothing more than to drop it right then and there. And you will work to never pick it up again. Because as the great Maya Angelou said, "Do the best you can until you know better. Then when you know better, do better."

Doing better is where other people come in. It's where you really begin to make a difference in the lives of others - by modeling self love and forgiveness and by being able to truly love other people. Other messed up, flawed people, like we all are. And you will be able to love the beautiful world we live in and help to make it a better place. For people. For animals and birds and fish and insects. For the mountains and valleys and oceans and streams. And for everyone who has yet to get here to enjoy this planet's magnificent beauty.

Up Your Love Game

LOVE YOURSELF BETTER

Some of us are pretty good at loving the other people in our lives. We take care of everyone else, leaving ourselves in last place time and time again. Here are a few simple ways to love yourself better:

- Respect your authentic self and your inner truth
- Surround yourself with people who love and appreciate YOU
- Choose to spend less time with people who sap your energy and bring down your spirit
- Stop comparing yourself to others (I mean it - comparison is the thief of joy)
- Don't say derogatory things about yourself to yourself
- Every now and again do something that is just for YOU
- Remind yourself of all the wonderful traits you possess
- And please, PLEASE stop "shoulding" all over yourself "I should do this, I should have done that." Just ... stop.

Up Your Love Game

BE A LIGHT IN THE WORLD

You know what happens when you up your love game and spread light and love in the world? You grow your love for yourself. You feel the love you share in your heart. Because love is miraculous, in whatever direction it is flowing!

- Make a difference somewhere - big or small
- Be your highest self
- Make a stranger's day - hold the door, give a compliment, let people pass on the freeway, show kindness
- Stand for what is right and true
- Be compassionate when others are struggling
- Serve where you are, give what you can
- Don't let the negative demand your attention - push it away by DOing something positive

Up Your Love Game

MAKING IT STICK - JOURNALING

What stood out for you in this chapter? What things do you plan to try or to do to up your love game?

Section Five: Joy Is All Around You

Joy. It seems so elusive sometimes. Hard to define. Even harder to capture and hold close.

Scientists define joy as an intense momentary experience of positive emotion - one that makes you smile, laugh and want to jump up and down. I like this definition. It makes me think of that video that resurfaces every once in a while on social media of the little dog so happy to see her master that she jumps up and down and does the doggie happy dance.

I believe there is another, less transitory, way to think of joy that works in harmony with the scientific definition. The joy that runs deep in our souls. The joy that connects us with the living world. The joy that knows that life is basically good and we are right where we are supposed to be at this exact moment. It is the well from which we are able to experience and appreciate the "pops" of joy in each day. And those little pops of joy add up.

Joy Is All Around You

UNIVERSALLY JOYFUL THINGS

Designer and TED presenter Ingrid Fetell Lee asked every-one she knew (and plenty of strangers) to share what brings them joy. She expected that most of the responses would be very specific and personal to the respondent. What she found, however, was that many people shared the exact same things over and over. Rainbows. Ice cream cones. Fireworks. Pops of bright color. Swimming pools. Bubbles. Hot air balloons. Confetti.

It seems like some things in the physical world are universally joyful. They can be seen and touched and experienced. There are little moments of joy hidden in plain sight if we know to look for them and savor them. And we can increase those pops of joy in our lives by consciously choosing to surround our-selves with what Fetell Lee calls the "aesthetics of joy."

"Scatter joy!"

Ralph Waldo Emerson

Joy Is All Around You

THE COLORS OF JOY

We might not be able to conjure up a rainbow in the sky but we can use its bright colors in our homes, offices and wardrobes to give us that spirit of joy.

Bright colors give us energy. Studies have shown that people who work in colorful spaces are more alert, more confident and friendlier than their counterparts in drab surroundings. People feel safer where there is color. Students learn better in a colorful space. So why do we so often surround ourselves with a washed-out color palette?

Black, white and gray is sophisticated and worldly, they say. Brown walls and furnishings are easier to match, they say. Bright-colored clothing is for children, they say. I say "they" are completely off-base. Color brings everyone joy and we could all use more of that in our lives. So bring on the yellow. And pink. And blue and green and every shade in between!

Joy Is All Around You

YOUR OWN "JOY SIGN"

I once worked with a wonderful and passionate woman who told me about her "joy sign" - a white limousine. For her, a white limo evoked a feeling of emotional and financial prosperity. It was a sign that she was on the right track to make all of her dreams come true. When she spotted a white stretch limo it gave her a pop of joy in her day. And once she started looking for them, she saw them everywhere!

Another woman I know lost her husband to cancer way too young. Her joy sign is a penny from heaven. When she finds a penny on the ground, she feels the joy of the love she shared with her beloved. It's a sign that he is still looking out for her and their daughter.

Do you have a joy sign?

Joy Is All Around You

MAKING IT STICK - JOURNALING

What stood out for you in this chapter? What things do you plan to try or to do to recognize the joy all around you?

_____
_____
_____
_____
_____
_____
_____
_____
_____
_____

Acknowledgments

Dreams may be unique to the dreamer but I have learned it
takes a lot of love and support to bring them to fruition.
I could write an entire book just thanking the people who
have brought so much joy, wisdom, help and love to my life!

First, my parents, Mel and Dorothy Hamre. Dad had a fun and
witty sense of humor and made everyone laugh. He was the
inventor of family fun night and "just come along for the ride."
Mom is our rock. She is wise, faith-filled, hard-working,
often silly and always kind. We laugh together and pray
together. Everyone who meets her adores her and I try my
best to be like her every day.

To my husband, Chuck Callahan (who is also my boyfriend,
my in-home IT guy, my nurse and pharmacist, my chef,
and my partner in the good and the bad, in sickness and in
health), my dreams are only truly possible because of you.
You brought never-ending love into my life and because
of you one of my deepest hopes came true - being a mom.
Thank you for loving me, trying to keep me well, and putting
up with my shenanigans.

To Jill Wagner - sister of my heart, collaborator, spiritual mentor and editor - thank you for helping me make this book finally happen.

To my family - brothers, sisters, nieces, nephews and the next generation of this crazy dynasty - thank you for all of your love, support, kindness and hospital visits! And to my beloved niece Lily, you may not realize this, but you saved me from my broken heart when it became clear I would not be able to have my own children. I treasure you and our very special relationship!

To Collin, the son of my heart, you give me so much joy and pride and happiness even (or especially) when you give me a hard time about pretty much everything.

To all of my fellow cancer warriors, caregivers and friends who have shared their hearts with me and graciously allowed me to share mine, thank you for uplifting me and helping me stay focused on the wonderful, positive things happening in the world every day.

And, finally, I owe my very life to a few amazing organizations whose staff and volunteers work tirelessly to eradicate blood cancer and help people going through their own challenging journeys. If you are looking for a charitable cause to support, these organizations are exceptional stewards:

- Be The Match   bethematch.org
- The Leukemia & Lymphoma Society   lls.org
- City of Hope   coh.org
- LifeStream Blood Bank   lstream.org

Resources

Chapman, Gary (2015). *The 5 Love Languages: The Secret to Love that Lasts* (Reprint). Northfield Publishing.

Fetell Lee, Ingrid (2018). *Joyful: The Surprising Power of Ordinary Things to Create Extraordinary Happiness*. Little, Brown Spark.

Lyubomirsky, Sonja (2008). *The How of Happiness: A New Approach to Getting the Life You Want*. Penguin Books.

Lyubomirsky, Sonja (2014). *The Myths of Happiness: What Should Make You Happy, but Doesn't, What Shouldn't Make You Happy, but Does*. Penguin Books.

Nelson, Shasta (2016). *Frientimacy: How to Deepen Friendships for Lifelong Health and Happiness*. Seal Press

Action For Happiness
www.actionforhappiness.org

Greater Good Science Center at UC Berkeley
https://greatergood.berkeley.edu

About the Author

Dianne Callahan is a motivational speaker, award-winning public relations professional, fundraising expert, author and 3-time cancer survivor. She lives in Southern California with her husband, Chuck, rescue dog Dagny, and two perfectly unimpressed cats, Sammy Joe and Precious.

Photo Credit: Michael Moody

Their daughter, Caitlin, is in grad school and son Collin lives in Washington, DC, with his wife, Megan. Dianne is patiently waiting for grandchildren.

To learn more about Dianne or to book her to speak at your event, visit www.LightheartedLife.org.

 www.facebook.com/ALightheartedLife

 www.pinterest.com/diannecallahan

 @lightheart_dc

 www.lightheartedlife.org

Made in the USA
San Bernardino, CA
14 November 2018